KU-706-682

THE 1916 RISING

EDWARD PURDON

ⓂERCIER PRESS

941·591/ 2402155.

POBLACHT NA H EIREANN.

THE PROVISIONAL GOVERNMENT
OF THE
IRISH REPUBLIC
TO THE PEOPLE OF IRELAND.

IRISHMEN AND IRISHWOMEN: In the name of God and of the dead generations from which she receives her old tradition of nationhood, Ireland, through us, summons her children to her flag and strikes for her freedom.

Having organised and trained her manhood through her secret revolutionary organisation, the Irish Republican Brotherhood, and through her open military organisations, the Irish Volunteers and the Irish Citizen Army, having patiently perfected her discipline, having resolutely waited for the right moment to reveal itself, she now seizes that moment, and, supported by her exiled children in America and by gallant allies in Europe, but relying in the first on her own strength, she strikes in full confidence of victory.

We declare the right of the people of Ireland to the ownership of Ireland, and to the unfettered control of Irish destinies, to be sovereign and indefeasible. The long usurpation of that right by a foreign people and government has not extinguished the right, nor can it ever be extinguished except by the destruction of the Irish people. In every generation the Irish people have asserted their right to national freedom and sovereignty: six times during the past three hundred years they have asserted it in arms. Standing on that fundamental right and again asserting it in arms in the face of the world, we hereby proclaim the Irish Republic as a Sovereign Independent State, and we pledge our lives and the lives of our comrades-in-arms to the cause of its freedom, of its welfare, and of its exaltation among the nations.

The Irish Republic is entitled to, and hereby claims, the allegiance of every Irishman and Irishwoman. The Republic guarantees religious and civil liberty, equal rights and equal opportunities to all its citizens, and declares its resolve to pursue the happiness and prosperity of the whole nation and of all its parts, cherishing all the children of the nation equally, and oblivious of the differences carefully fostered by an alien government, which have divided a minority from the majority in the past.

Until our arms have brought the opportune moment for the establishment of a permanent National Government, representative of the whole people of Ireland and elected by the suffrages of all her men and women, the Provisional Government, hereby constituted, will administer the civil and military affairs of the Republic in trust for the people.

We place the cause of the Irish Republic under the protection of the Most High God, Whose blessing we invoke upon our arms, and we pray that no one who serves that cause will dishonour it by cowardice, inhumanity, or rapine. In this supreme hour the Irish nation must, by its valour and discipline and by the readiness of its children to sacrifice themselves for the common good, prove itself worthy of the august destiny to which it is called.

Signed on Behalf of the Provisional Government,

THOMAS J. CLARKE.
SEAN Mac DIARMADA,   THOMAS MacDONAGH,
P. H. PEARSE,   EAMONN CEANNT,
JAMES CONNOLLY.   JOSEPH PLUNKETT.

Leabharlann Contae na Midhe

The Proclamation read aloud by Patrick Pearse outside the GPO on Easter Monday

CONTENTS

1

THE RED-GOLD FLAME

I remember once as a boy half-learning a patriotic song called 'Who Fears to Speak of Easter Week?' It was written anonymously by a nun in flattering imitation of 'The Memory of the Dead', the famous Ninety-Eighty ballad of John Kells Ingram (1823–1907), and began with the quatrain:

> Who fears to speak of Easter Week?
> Who does its fate deplore?
> The red-gold fame of Ireland's name
> Confronts the world once more!

It was written some time after the executions of the leaders of the Easter Rising perhaps during the Anglo-Irish War of 1919–21, when patriotism for a majority of people, especially outside of Ulster, had become pure and simple.

Both before or after those two-and-a-half years the response to 1916 would have considerably more muddied. The general reaction to the events of Easter Week, as will become clear, was far from enthusiastic throughout the nationalist community. Yet a majority of these people whose reactions varied from rage to hatred would suffer a remarkable change in the weeks and months after Pearse's unconditional surrender at Great Britain Street (as Parnell Street was then called) at 3.30 p.m. on Saturday, 29 April 1916 to Brigadier-General W. H. M. Lowe. Those who had witnessed the drilling and marching with interest or derision for nearly a year were surprised at the outbreak of fighting and many who watched the volunteers march to their imprisonment in the Rotunda grounds in what seemed like ignominy were soon to cease their mockery and become part of the struggle.

Part of the anger shown by the Dublin citizens originated in the fact that many had fathers, brothers, sons and uncles fighting in the Great War in Irish regiments for a number of reasons, mainly economic, a good number believing that their participation in the 'war to end wars' was to be ultimately for the benefit of their own 'small nation'. Such irreproachable patriots as Arthur Griffith (1871–1922), founder of Sinn Féin, Bulmer Hobson (1883–69), writer and member of the Irish Republican Brotherhood (IRB); Thomas Kettle (1880–1916), poet, essayist and nationalist MP; Francis Ledwidge (1887–1917) poet and trades union organiser; Robert Lynd (1879–1949), nationalist journalist, essayist and critic, and friend of James Connolly; John Redmond (1856–1918), the leader of the Home Rule party and his deputy John Dillon (1851–1927) were horrified to hear of the occupation of the GPO, City Hall, Boland's Mills and the other not particularly strategic buildings on Easter Monday, 24 April and felt betrayed that the constitutional and non-violent strategies of the nationalist and Sinn Féin parties which had seemed to successful had been betrayed.

The mixture of dismay and ribaldry that greeted the rising in the city was muted compared with the general surprise. Yeats's famous poem 'Easter 1916', published in *Michael Robartes and the Dancer* (1922) underscores this mixture of bewilderment and mockery:

> Being certain that they and I
> But lived where motley is worn:
> All's changed, changed utterly
> A terrible beauty is born.

The main reason for the bewilderment was that armed rising was considered a thing of the past; *pace* the enthusiasm of the reverend balladeer, 'the red glow flame of Ireland's name' had barely flickered for more that a century.

The United Irishmen, rising in the summer of 1798, the 'Year of Liberty' with short-lived forays in Antrim, Down, Carlow, Dublin, Mayo and a more effective and longer-lasting insurrection in Wexford was a kind of waking from a long sleep but apart from a kind of limited affray such as Robert Emmet's premature adventure in Dublin in July 1803 the nineteenth century was relatively quiet. The tithe wars of the 1830s and the continuing agrarian outrages of the secret societies though locally bloody did not amount to world-shaking events. The Young Irelanders led by William Smith O'Brien

(1803–64) – the 'Middle-Aged Irelander' as he called himself – after the death of Thomas Davis (1814–45) had a risibly unsuccessful and largely bloodless rebellion in 1848 and the Fenians in the 1860s were not much more effective. The Smith O'Brien rising had co-incided with the worst year of the Great Famine and the country had changed completely by the time the Fenian Brotherhood were making so much noise in Canada, Manchester and Clerken-well. Political activity under Isaac Butt (1813–79), Charles Stewart Parnell (1846–91) and John Redmond had been generally constitutional and non-violent, though some of the events of the Land War had been bloody, and aberrations like the murder of Lord Frederick Cavendish, the newly-appointed chief secretary and the under-secretary T. H. Burke, by the Invincibles (an extremist society with Fenian connections) in May 1882 were not unknown.

This sense of inactivity was put succinctly by Roger Casement, one of the significant players in the Rising, in a letter written from Germany to his friend Joe McGarrity of Clan na Gael in April 1915:

> So far the mass of the exponents of Irish nationality have contented themselves for over a century with deeds not words.

The Fenian movement did, however, generate two organisations which were to play significant parts in events nearly sixty years later: the IRB and Clan na Gael. The second of these was based in America and by 1870 had 10,000 members. It came under the leadership of John Devoy (1842–1928), a Fenian from County Kildare, who after five years of imprisonment had emigrated to America in 1871. He had played an important part in the Land League agitation of the 1880s and was a sponsor of the Easter Rising, which could be considered as an IRB manifestation even if only a fraction of a fraction of its members were involved. Links had been established by the Americans with this generally disorganised association by 1880 and though it was largely inactive during the leadership of Parnell and the Parliamentary Party it had a renascence in the first decade of the new century when the vacuum caused by the leader's fall and death (1890–1) was filled with a variety of political movements.

Though there was no significant armed revolt during the nineteenth-century there had nevertheless been generated a revolutionary iconography with its own sacred texts. Ninety-Eight had produced contemporary broadsheet ballads and the columns of *The Nation (1842-8)*, the organ of Young Ireland, were filled up with literary ones such as 'The Memory of the Dead' and 'The Croppy Boy' by William McBurney (1844–92). The centenary of 1798 had produced many more. The celebrations at home and in America and Australia had passed off peacefully but the implicit approval of the aims of the revolutionaries and the enthusiastic singing of such ballads as 'Boolavogue' and 'The Boys of Wexford' showed that there was still a sentimental (if safe) attachment to what was for many the 'old cause'. 'Bold Robert Emmet' apart from being the subject of a popular turn-of-the century ballad and the protagonist of a popular 'drama' as played by travelling companies and many amateur societies, had also left a much-quoted 'speech from the dock'.

Most significant in light of later claims was

the Fenian oath which was taken by all members of both the IRB and Clan Na Gael:

> I do solemnly swear allegiance to the Irish Republic, now virtually established; that I will take up arms at a moment's notice to defend its integrity and independence; that I will yield implicit obedience to the commands of my superior, and finally I take this oath in the spirit of the true soldier of liberty. So help me, God.

The words 'now virtually established' formed the basis for all subsequent claims of paramilitaries that what they were conducting was a war, the authority of the notional republic being the basis for their moral stance.

The tremendous popularity of Lady Gregory's play *The Rising of the Moon* (1907), about the innate nationalism of an RIC sergeant, and of *Cathleen Ni Houlihan*, the 1798 play that Yeats wrote in 1902 for his revolutionary English love Maud Gonne (both in their time members of the IRB) showed that there was a living tradition which did not look unkindly on past rebellions, whatever their feelings about a twentieth-century one. Stephen Gwynn (1864–1950), the Protestant nationalist MP and grandson of Smith O'Brien, wrote after seeing Maud Gonne in the play, 'I went home asking myself if such plays should be produced unless one was prepared to go out and shoot and be shot.' Yeats too wondered in the year of his death:

> Did that play of mine send out
> Certain men the English shot?

Apart from the raising of nationalist awareness brought about by the centenary and the conscious Irishness of the Literary Revival there was also in existence two overtly non-political institutions that played a similar part in the rise of the 'new nationalism'. These were the Gaelic Athletic Association and the Gaelic League and both were deliberate asserters of non-English Irishness. The first, begun in 1884 by Michael Cusack (1847–1906), may very well have been a deliberate initiative by the Fenian movement, specifically organised through the impressionable

Cusack by the IRB. Its purpose was the fostering of Gaelic games and the banning of English ones (and the refusal of entry to all security forces, even the RIC) and certainly by the end of the first decade of the new century its membership was strongly IRB-influenced. The Gaelic League was established in 1893 for the purpose of restoring Irish as a literary and spoken language by a County Antrim Catholic Eoin MacNeill (1967–1945), a court clerk and self-taught scholar, and Douglas Hyde (1860–1949) the son of a Connacht clergyman who the previous year had given his inaugural address as president of the National Literary Society on the subject of 'The Necessity for De-anglicizing the Irish People'.

Both these institutions were eventually effective in their stated aims and both became highly politicised. By 1915 the patently revolutionary aims of such members of the League as Patrick Pearse and MacNeill made it impossible for Hyde to remain. For most of the first twenty years of its existence it had had a considerable number of Protestant – and even unionist – members but after 'The North Began', MacNeill's article written for the League's journal *An Claidheamh Soluis* (1899–1918) about the gunrunning of the Ulster Volunteer Force (UVF) in 1912 and the resultant formation of the Irish Volunteers, it could not in any sense be regarded as non-political.

There was, then, at least an emotional awareness of a kind of historical precedent for what has since become known as the 'armed struggle' but nothing was further from the intentions of the men of 1916 than a prolonged attrition. The rationale was expressed by Pearse in one of his poems as 'bloody protest for a glorious thing' and Yeats, understanding if not approving the gesture, put it well in 'The Rose Tree', written a year after the rising, and consisting of an imagined dialogue between Pearse and Connolly:

'There nothing but our own red blood
Can make a right rose tree.'

All of this was clear in retrospect but few people even among the participants could have known what 'that delirium of the brave' would bring about.

2

IRISH VOLUNTEERS
AND CITIZEN ARMY

Though speculation about 'What might have happened in history if . . . ?' is the vainest of parlour games, it is possible that the perceived need for a gesture of military action, which was all the Easter Rising could hope to be, would never have arisen if the Liberal government had been able to face down the intransigence of unionist opposition to what they called with only minimal justification Rome Rule. The impasse had begun to solidify as early as 1912. In response to the Home Rule Bill's being presented to the Commons on 11 April of that year, 218,000 Northern Protestants signed the Solemn League and Covenant. On Ulster Day (28 September) supported by Bonar Law (1858–1923) in Westminster and led at home by the Dublin lawyer Edward Carson (1854–1935)

and the Belfast distiller James Craig (1871–
1940) they pledged 'to use all means to prevent
the present conspiracy . . . '

Already thanks to the network of Orange
and other lodges they had established the Ulster
Volunteer Force which was to be armed with
35,000 German rifles landed 'illegally' (but with
police connivance) at Larne, Bangor and Don-
aghadee in April 1914, exactly a month before
the Bill was finally carried. The attitude of the
British Army had become clear in March in the
Curragh Incident when General Gough persuaded fifty-seven out of seventy officers to
resign their commissions rather than enforce
Home Rule in Ulster. A bitter civil war seemed
inevitable and the only alternative was partition.
The nature of this secession was proving to be
as impossible of resolution as any other question
involving the well-supported unionists who were
as so often before pawns in a bitter game of
Westminster politics. The Tory party had often
found it advantageous to 'play the Orange card'
in the words of Lord Randolph Churchill, the
dead father of the Liberal government's First
Lord of the Admiralty, and this was to prove to

be the most deadly trick in the game. The Buckingham Palace conference of July 1914 called by George V (reasonably assumed to be on the side of the 'disloyalists') had solved nothing when on 4 August Germany invaded Belgium and to everyone's relief the matter was postponed until 'the end of hostilities' which even the army knew would be around Christmas!

The founding of the UVF had not gone unnoticed outside of the four unionist counties of Down, Antrim, Armagh and Derry, nor had the successful gun-running by the *Clydevalley*. Michael Joseph O'Rahilly (1875–1916), a Kerry journalist who called himself 'the O'Rahilly' and expected others to do so too, became editor of *An Claidheamh Soluis* in 1913 and set about refurbishing it. He asked MacNeill for an editorial for the first issue of 1 November 1913 and got 'The North Began', effectively an admonition that Home Rulers should follow the Unionists' example and set up their own armed Irish Volunteers. Three weeks later on 25 November at the Rotunda rink, out of doors because of the numbers, that militia was set up with a strong involvement of the now buoyant if minuscule IRB.

Branches were established throughout the country with, hardly surprisingly, the strongest response in Ulster. This was partly due to the organising ability of Hobson and his IRB colleague Denis McCullough (1883–1968) and partly because northern nationalists not for the first time, nor the last, felt particularly isolated and vulnerable. Redmond was slow at first to support the movement but by 14 June 1914 on being allowed to nominate half the seats on the committee had given his consent and the numbers rose to 160,000. *Their* arms running was not blinked at by the authorities. Fifteen hundred guns were landed at Howth from the *Asgard* (navigated by Erskine Childers) on 26 July 1914. The King's Own Scottish Borderers, returning to barracks, having failed to seize the guns, fired on a jeering crowd in Bachelor's Walk, killing four and wounding thirty-seven. There were also many baton charges by a force of the Dublin Metropolitan Police (DMP). The incident, though caused by fatigue and misunderstood orders, shocked the nationalist population. Augustine Birrell, the genial and diplomatic chief secretary, set up a commission which found, within a fortnight, that the action of the police and army had been 'tainted with illegality' and Birrell sacked the Assistant-Commissioner of the DMP. The damage was done and it was believed that the official attitude to nationalists was rather different from that to Ulster Protestants.

Birrell was a clever and liberal secretary, a man of culture and a successful belletrist. His handling of affairs in Ireland was subtle and effective, maintaining close links with Redmond and Dillon, and allowing the Volunteers a lot of latitude. He did not regard them as harmless idealists, as his dispatches to the cabinet show, but he was determined not to make martyrs of them. If he was taken by surprise by the events of Easter Monday 1916 it was only because he had read MacNeill's public announcement of the cancelling of manoeuvres in the *Sunday Independent*. His perhaps inevitable resignation on 3 May, the day of the first executions, meant that affairs in Ireland were to be handled at a distance by the Home Secretary, which meant in practice disastrous martial law, administered by a martinet.

John Redmond had led the parliamentary party well and it had seemed that he was about to succeed where his uncrowned king had failed, but without real support from Asquith and Lloyd George he had little hope of handling the unionists. The outbreak of hostilities was a kind of relief even for him. He called for the same support for the war effort as the members of the Ulster division had shown in the North – only after they had been assured that the Home Rule Bill had definitely been postponed – and he got it for a number of reasons, not all political. The original Rotunda-rink members numbering at most 3,000 broke away, calling themselves the *Irish* Volunteers, as opposed to Redmond's *National* Volunteers. With MacNeill as chief of staff the leaders began to recruit supporters so that by 1916 they could count on 15,000 members. MacNeill was on the whole against a military initiative, except in the extreme case of the Volunteers' being suppressed and this was taken to be the policy of the movement as a whole. They were to be made into an effective army so that there would be no doubts about the Home Rule Bill's being implemented. Besides,

as a good Catholic and a pragmatist the only
rising MacNeill would countenance would be
one with a chance of success.

The outbreak of war, however, was regarded
by the IRB as a clear example of the old Fenian
dictum: England's difficulty; Ireland's opportunity. It also called to mind the prayer of the
fiery Young Irelander, John Mitchel (1815–75)
who had written in his *Jail Journal* (1854) 'Send
war in our time, O Lord!' Yet it was still a tiny
organisation rekindled in Ireland mainly by the
old Fenian Tom Clarke, who had been sent
home in 1907 by Devoy for that purpose. His
tobacconist shop in Great Britain Street became
the centre of IRB activity and he found a
resourceful colleague in Sean MacDermott who
had joined the organisation in Belfast through
his friendship with Hobson and McCullough.
Like them he broke with Arthur Griffith's Sinn
Féin (founded with Hobson in 1905), one of the
more successful alternatives to Redmond's consti-
tutionalism, because of its gradualism and
advocacy of passive resistance.

The need for a gesture, maybe even martyr-
dom, was to be formulated by Patrick Pearse,

who though also a devout Catholic felt that the justice of the IRB's cause superseded the conventional teaching of the Church. This required that for a rebellion to be legitimate a number of criteria be met: the government must be tyrannical; the community as a whole must approve; the tyranny be removable only by bloodshed and its evil be greater than the effects of the revolution; that it should have a likely chance of success. Even the most sanguine of the IRB knew that none of these conditions were met. The horrors of the European war in which thousands were dying every day made the life of young men seem cheap. The spirit of those British who flocked to recruiting stations in August 1914, exemplified in Rupert Brooke's poem 'If I Should Die . . .' was not all that far removed from Pearse's: 'The old heart of the earth needed to be warmed with the red wine of the battlefields.'

Less clear was the motivation of the two who coopted Pearse on to a military committee in 1915: Tom Clarke and Sean MacDermott, his austere lieutenant. Clarke had been a revolutionary, a member of Clan na Gael since the age of twenty-one, and had been imprisoned as a dynamitard. Perhaps he too felt that a gallant gesture, which was all any rising might be, would in time produce the effect the Fenian tradition required. The symbol of the phoenix, so dear to the movement, implied immolation. The impenetrable MacDermott who battled with poliomyelitis and suffered imprisonment under the Defence of the Realm Acts (DORA), the emergency wartime legislation, for anti-recruiting activities, continued with IRB organisation for which he had a special and fanatical talent.

The most hard-headed of the 1916 leaders was James Connolly and as trades union organiser and a Marxist intellectual the least likely to be won over by Pearse's sacrificial mysticism. Yet he too began making the same kind of noises about the need for an armed rising while the European war lasted. He was a socialist, the able lieutenant of James Larkin (1876–1947) in the Irish Transport and General Workers Union (ITGWU). He had taken over control during the infamous Dublin lock-out of 1913 and formed the Irish Citizen Army as a kind of rapid response unit to protect pickets from the often violent irruptions of the sabre-wielding DMP. Its numbers were small, not more than 350, and mostly union members, and its spite of its socialist character sufficiently nationalistic to want self-determination for Ireland. Among its more colourful members were the rebel Countess Markievicz (née Constance Gore-Booth) and the playwright Sean O'Casey who resigned when she joined. Connolly believed that though his force was small once word of an outbreak became known the whole country would rise. With the innocence of a doctrinaire Marxist he also held that a capitalist society would never destroy its own property by shelling.

When it became clear that Connolly might well initiate an independent outbreak he was invited to meet the members of the military council of the IRB. He was not seen for three days in the January of 1916 and afterwards it was obvious that he had been apprised of the council's intention to rise at Easter and that he was to be part of it. The committee now consisted of Pearse, Joseph Plunkett, Thomas MacDonagh, Clarke, Eamonn Ceannt and MacDermott and part of their strategy was to deceive MacNeill. They also kept Denis McCullough, who according to the IRB constitution was president of the Irish Republic, in the dark about their intentions. MacNeill would still not countenance Volunteer involvement in any 'act of rash violence'. They would keep in readiness for their future purpose of imposing, if necessary, the limited Home Rule offered by Asquith's bill. Only the threat of its suppression or conscription in the British Army would make him change his mind.

On the Wednesday of Holy Week 1916 he was given the proof he needed that suppression was imminent. A document giving details of the authorities' intention to arrest Volunteer leaders was read out at a meeting of Dublin Corporation by a councillor. He immediately ordered that the Volunteers should prepare themselves for resistance but not, he insisted, for insurrection. (The complicated moves of deception were cleverly orchestrated by MacDermott and it was he who arranged that Bulmer Hobson, who had argued all along against what Pearse and his colleagues were advocating, should be kidnapped and held incommunicado for the three vital days from the evening of Good Friday until the rising was a fact on Easter Monday.)

MacNeill was almost won over to the IRB plan especially when he was told by MacDermott that a large consignment of arms was on its way from Germany. MacDermott, convinced that MacNeill (though required for mobilisation purposes as titular head of the Volunteers) was a block to the adamant intention of the military council, tried to undermine his position by hinting that he had resigned. He had not. On Holy Saturday he learned that the Castle document was a forgery prepared by MacDermott and Plunkett and that the ship with the German guns had scuttled itself in Queenstown Harbour. He at once countermanded any orders that might have been received by Volunteers about the Easter weekend and put the advertisement in the *Sunday Independent* as confirmation.

The only effect was to postpone the rising by a day.

3

THE PROCLAMATION

One of the most dramatic moments in what was a generally untheatrical week was one of the first: the reading on the steps of the GPO in Sackville Street of the proclamation by Pearse and its subsequent pasting to the wall. The 500-word document is a fine piece of rhetoric and in its restraint and lack of quasi-religious emotionalism (except in the apostrophe to the Most High God in the final paragraph) not entirely the work of Pearse himself. It claimed the Rising as an IRB gesture, a means of recovering the phoenix flame after the farce of '67 but it also associated with the IRB the Volunteers and the Citizen Army. This was a large claim since relatively few members of these bodies were involved. The Rising was not so much a minority happening as one involving a minority of three minorities.

It was sociologically ahead of its time in its suggestion of a welfare state and feminist in its stated equality of the sexes, a clear indication of input by Connolly. Its tone was remarkably in contrast to the attitudes of the Volunteers as a whole, whose rhetoric emphasised 'manly' deeds and tended to patronise the members of Cumann na mBan (its auxiliary corps set up in 1914) as earlier Sinn Féin had seemed condescending, in the language of the *Zeitgeist*, towards its older sororial organisation Inghinidhe na hÉireann. (set up by Maud Gonne in 1900). It recognised that the women involved (over ninety with sixty from Cumann na mBan) were sharing the risks of the men and though they on the whole took no part in the actual fighting they were used for the much more dangerous job of dispatch-carrying, as well as serving as field nurses and cooks.

The seven signatories were taking upon themselves the ultimate responsibility and all had a pretty clear idea of what the outcome would be for them at any rate. Because of the myth-making, not to say hagiography, that tended to characterise accounts of the Rising, at least for the first fifty years, it is difficult for those who grew up with the myth to realise that the signatories and the other men made famous by their deaths were relatively unknown even in the notoriously village-city that was the Dublin of the time. Yeats may have met them with vivid faces but they were coming from counter or desk.

Pearse (b. 1879) had become a barrister but his only recorded case, which he lost, was in the defence of a Donegal man who had contravened the regulations by having his name in Irish on his cart. He was chiefly known as a writer, Gaelic activist and education theorist who had found his own school, St Enda's in Ranelagh, later moving to Rathfarnham. Ceannt (b. 1881) was a corporation clerk and chiefly famous for having played the uileann pipes for Pius X at his golden jubilee in 1908. MacDermott (b.1881) – who signed himself Seán MacDiarmada – had been a tram conductor and was the longest serving member of the IRB apart from Clarke (b. 1857). Plunkett (b. 1887), the youngest of the signatories, was the son of a hereditary papal

Roger Casement (left) and John Devoy, who helped Casement make contact with the German authorities, in New York, 1914

Members of the Irish Citizen Army on the roof of Liberty Hall, the headquarters of the Transport Union (National Museum of Ireland)

'The Birth of the Republic,' by Walter Paget, depicts events inside
the GPO towards the end of the Rising

WOODTOWN PARK.
RATHFARNHAM,
CO. DUBLIN.

22 apl 1916

Volunteers completely
deceived. All orders for
tomorrow Sunday are
entirely cancelled.
Eóinmacnéill

An order issued by Eoin MacNeill two days before the Rising. It
reads 'Volunteers completely deceived. All orders for tomorow
Sunday are entirely cancelled.'
(National Museum of Ireland)

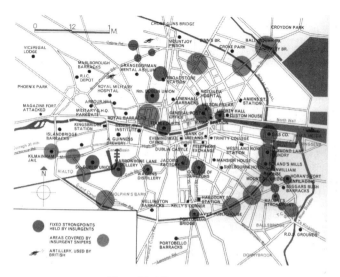

Map of Dublin, Easter 1916

Patrick Pearse surrendering to General Lowe, 29 April 1916
(National Museum of Ireland)

Execution scene, Kilmainham Jail, May 1916
Artist unknown (National Museum of Ireland)

count and found it necessary to travel for health reason but had been a prominent figure in Dublin literary circles. The best known were MacDonagh (b. 1878) and Connolly (b.1868) but for strikingly different reasons. MacDonagh was a poet, playwright and academic critic and a lecturer in English in UCD; Connolly had been an effective and unpopular ITGWU official in Belfast and either loved or execrated as Larkin's deputy. Of the others who died Willie Pearse (b.1881), brother of Patrick, was a sculptor and art teacher in St Enda's; Edward Daly (b.1891), brother-in-law of Tom Clarke, had worked in a bakery and wholesale chemist; Michael O'Hanrahan (b. 1877) was a journalist and Michael Mallin (b. 1880) a silk weaver; Con Colbert (b. 1888) also worked in a bakery; Sean Heuston (b.1891) had been a railway worker; John MacBride (b. 1865), famous as the estranged husband of Maud Gonne, had fought for the Boers and was employed by Dublin Waterworks; Tom Kent (b. c. 1867) who was shot in Cork military detention barracks after surrender in a gun battle had been a farmer. Eamon de Valera (b. 1882) the only leader to escape the firing-squad, because of Redmond's intervention with Asquith, had been a lecturer in mathematics. The rebellion was neither plebeian nor bourgeois but drew its participants from a vertical section through the Irish society of the time.

Pearse was the main rhetorician who found the words to express the particular sacrifice that the small band of patriots were about to make. A poem entitled 'Christmas 1915' reads:

O King that was born
To set bondsmen free,
In the coming battle,
Help the Gael.

And his funeral oration at the grave of the old Fenian, O'Donovan Rossa, in Glasnevin on 1 August 1915, though scarcely heard because of the crowds, the presence of a larger armed force of Redmond's National Volunteers (there because O'Donovan Rossa for the last years of his life was if anything a Redmondite) and his own poor delivery, became a sacred text. It reiterated his conviction: 'Life springs from death; and from the graves of patriot men and women spring living nations' and its peroration was the inflammatory: 'The fools, the fools, the fools! – they have left us our Fenian dead, and while Ireland holds these graves, Ireland unfree shall never be at peace!'

One of the mantras that has come down from the time is 'Sixteen Dead Men', the title of another poem about the Rising by Yeats who by the time of writing was happy to be accounted if not true brother of this company too, then at least a close relation. The sixteenth was not shot but hanged as a traitor in Pentonville Prison, London on 3 August and the phrase from the proclamation, 'gallant allies in Europe' was a vain tribute to the work he had tried to do. This was Roger Casement (b. 1864), who was brought up in County Antrim and having joined the British consular service in 1895 was knighted for humanitarian services because of reports of mistreatment of native workers in the Congo and South America. He was always of strong nationalist sympathies and having joined the Volunteers argued that the only hope of a successful rising lay with German guns and an

Irish brigade of prisoners-of-war.

He made his way to Berlin from New York in 1914 and travelled to Limburg, near Koblenz where the German authorities, only too anxious to cooperate with an enemy of England and no doubt thinking, 'England's difficulty is Germany's opportunity', had collected 2,000 Irish prisoners. He was unsuccessful in establishing the Irish brigade and generally got a poor reception. He was not an ideal recruiting officer, his neuroticism imperfectly concealed. The Germans were naturally disappointed since their support for a possible rising was anti-British rather than pro-Irish. Casement remained in Germany, 'a virtual prisoner' and unwell most of the time.

Plunkett was sent in April 1915 by the usual circuitous route through neutral countries to tell Casement about the IRB's plans and to sue for 50,000 rifles and ammunition. Casement advised him that no rising should take place, especially when their German contacts refused their request and advised them that they should look to America where there were millions of Irishmen with money to supply their needs. There was to be no Irish brigade and the IRB military council should be so informed; it is believed that Plunkett did not deliver the message but in view of the mind-set of the inner council it would have been ignored anyway. In February 1916 Devoy through the German ambassador in Washington asked the German High Command for 100,000 rifles, for artillery and German officers. All the Germans offered were 20,000 rifles (captured from Russia on the eastern front), ten machine guns and five million rounds. These would be landed in Kerry and distributed to the Volunteers in Munster and Connacht in preparation for a simultaneous revolt. Casement knew this shipment to be totally inadequate and made his way to Ireland to insist that the Rising be called off. He travelled on the U-19, the submarine escort of the arms ship the *Libau*, which was masquerading as a Norwegian trawler the *Aud*.

The *Aud* eluded the British blockade and appeared in Tralee Bay on Holy Thursday, four days early than the arranged rendezvous. She waited twenty-four hours for some signal and then, intercepted by the Royal Navy, was being escorted into Queenstown when the captain,

Karl Spindler scuttled the ship with the German flag flying. That same day, Good Friday, Casement nearly drowned as his dinghy capsized on Banna Strand and later, exhausted and dispirited, he was arrested and taken to Tralee. There would be neither arms nor men from the gallant allies in Europe but nothing was going to stop the IRB's bloody sacrifice.

4

EASTER WEEK

The number who turned out was about 1,500, consisting of Volunteers, Citizen Army, Cumann na mBan, and Fianna Éireann (the National boy scouts). The majority (including Pearse, Connolly, Clarke, MacDermott and Plunkett) occupied the General Post Office in Sackville Street as headquarters. (Their taking over was not without a certain comedy in that at least one customer insisted on completing his purchase of stamps before leaving.) A group known as the 1st Battalion Irish Volunteers, led by Commandant Edward Daly, occupied the Four Courts and set up posts at Jameson's distillery and various buildings in the Church Street-North King Street area. The Mendicity Institute across the Liffey on Usher's Island, was taken over by D Company under the command of

Captain Sean Heuston. MacDonagh, in charge of the 2nd Battalion, took over Jacob's biscuit factory in Bishop Street near St Stephen's Green, which had been occupied by Mallin of the Citizen Army with Countess Markievicz as second-in-command. Boland's bakery and flour mill were taken by de Valera and he set up outposts on the railway between Westland Row and Lansdowne Road at Mount Street Bridge on the Grand Canal. Ceannt with Cathal Brugha took over the South Dublin Union with deployments at Marrowbone Lane, Ardee Street and Cork Street. Sean Connolly, one of the first casualties, and a company of Citizen Army members occupied the City Hall.

The emplacements formed a rough ring around the GPO headquarters and were placed near some of the British barracks. In fact Beggar's Bush barracks was effectively unmanned, as was Dublin Castle. Trinity College with its thick sixteenth-century walls was virtually empty of students or soldiers. The original strategy was devised by Plunkett, now very ill, and Connolly, and seemed to consist of holding out until spontaneous risings west of the Shannon would seize most of Munster and Connacht and personnel then march on the capital. Without the promised arms from Germany and given the welter of command and counter-command this could not happen. Clarke, however, believed that they could withstand counterattack for months, by which time the war would surely be over and the IRB have its place at a post-war conference table. The failure of nerve at the Castle was an indication of military inexperience and it was characteristic that Sean Connolly was shot raising a flag on buildings opposite. Another example of military incompetence was the failure to cut all communications. Though the total number of troops in the city was about 1,200, reinforcements were soon on their way from Belfast, the Curragh, Templemore and Athlone, summoned by telephone.

The first incident occurred in Phoenix Park when a body of Volunteers, having set out even before the reading of the Proclamation, failed to blow up the arms dump at the Magazine Fort. The first casualty was the seventeen-year-old son of the fort's commander who was shot as he tried to reach a telephone to raise the alarm. The unarmed DMP sergeant on duty at the outer gate of the Castle was another early casualty but the full bitterness of what any violent rising may mean was not understood until four o'clock when a band of the Irish Volunteer Defence Corps, a middle-aged group of Irishmen forming a reserve group of the British Army, were attacked as they were returning to Beggar's Bush after a route march. These, known locally as the Gorgeous Wrecks from the 'GR' they wore on their armbands and carrying unloaded rifles, were raked with bullets. Five died and nine were wounded.

The first tactical manoeuvre (in an adventure that saw few) was made by Mallin and Markievicz when they realised that St Stephen's Green was vulnerable to fire from the Shelbourne Hotel on the north side and that their digging of trenches had been a waste of effort. They took over the Royal College of Surgeons on the west side but were driven out by reinforced British fire on the next afternoon. The only serious activity from the GPO headquarters was the shooting of four Lancers in Sackville Street on that Monday afternoon. The first soldiers to engage the rebels were from the Dublin Fusiliers and the Royal Irish Rifles but already a mob of Dubliners, alert to the fact that the police had been withdrawn, had begun looting from the fashionable stores in Sackville Street. Someone said that the reading of the proclamation at 12.45 by Pearse, not a great speaker at the best of times, was drowned out by the sound of breaking glass.

By the coming of night in what had been a fine sunny spring day the crowds from Fairyhouse races and other Bank Holiday treats returned to a terribly changed Dublin. The death roll included civilians as well as Volunteers, police and soldiers. The moods of amusement, bemusement and perplexity had hardened to rage and hatred. The Irish, then as now, had sufficient political awareness to understand that what had been agreed national policy and implied the deaths of many of the countrymen in Flanders was being challenged and perhaps eroded. One eye-witness of the time recorded in *Curious Journey*, the oral history compiled by Kenneth Griffith and Timothy O'Grady, describes how when he arrived at Jacob's on the Tuesday morning, 'the place was surrounded by a howling mob roaring at the Volunteers inside, "Come out to France and fight you lot of so-and-so slackers."'

Over the Post Office flew two strange flags, one green with the words Irish Republic painted in gold, and a tricolour of green, white and orange, another gesture of wishful thinking in its implicit idea of reconciliation, a relic of Young Ireland. Above the roof of the Imperial Hotel flew the Citizen Army flag: a plough with a sword on its coulter and decked with seven stars. It socialist credentials were impeccable but it was to give a title to a play which in its emotional truth about Easter Week was to prove unpalatable to the post-revolutionary audiences.

By Tuesday General Lowe had declared martial law in Dublin city and county, having now 5,000 troops at his disposal. His strategy was to keep an unbreachable line of troops along an east-west axis that would separate the posts on the north side of the Liffey, including the GPO headquarters, from the rest. He soon recovered control of a line between Kingsbridge Station and Trinity. He also had four pieces of artillery which came from Athlone and were set up near Prussia Street and in Phibsborough above the Cabra Road. It was typical of the informal nature of the affair that a private in the Dublin Fusiliers could stop a Volunteer friend in Dorset Street to warn him that the guns were on the way and to get the message to the GPO. The shelling began and continued for the rest of the week, gradually destroying the buildings in the centre of the city and showing no regard for capitalist principles. It did increase the anger of the populace and made looting somewhat more hazardous.

That day the Citizen Army battalion came under such fire from the Shelbourne and the United Services Club that they were forced to abandon their position in the College of Surgeons. A four-page newspaper called the *Irish War News* was printed in Liberty Hall and had optimistic news that 'The Republican forces hold the lines taken up at twelve noon on Easter Monday, and nowhere, despite fierce and almost continuous attacks of the British forces, have the lines been broken through.' It also urged civilians to build barricades in the streets to oppose the advance of the British troops – in other words to invite death while totally unarmed. The equality principles of the proclamation had slipped somewhat:

> There is work for everyone; for the men
> in the fighting line, and for the women
> in the provision of food and first aid.

The main roles for the women volunteers were as the *War News* described them. There were sixty from *Cumann na mBan* and they catered and cared for the men in the various posts. Their services were not always appreciated nor were they all equally skilled. *Curious Journey* recalls an occasion in the Four Courts kitchen when they made tea by putting a pound of the dry leaves into the water left over from boiling turnips. The result was indescribable and Sean Howard, the man who took the first mouthful, cried, 'Well you're Cumann na mBan maybe, but it's Cumann na Monsters you are. You want to kill us off.' (The book also records that Howard was shot the next day while carrying a dispatch to Piaras Beaslaí in the Father Matthew Hall in

Church Street.) One commander refused to allow any women into his post. This was de Valera and long afterwards he offended one of the women of 1916, the feminist and suffragist Hanna Sheehy-Skeffington, by confiding that it was probably a mistake since he had to release some of his men for the 'womanly' tasks of nursing and making meals.

By now, although there were no newspapers, the word was getting out that something unusual was happening in Dublin. Some Volunteers tried to get to Dublin, in spite of MacNeill's prohibition, but found it impossible to get near the rebel posts. The Volunteers were strong in Tyrone and when the word came of events in Dublin they turned out in Carrickmore in pouring rain; Donaghmore and Coalisland waited for orders and did not mobilise until the Tuesday morning at 11 o'clock but went home again, their leader Dr Patrick McCartan (1878–1963) having to hide out in a barn in the Sperrins. There was a similar inconclusive mustering of 132 men in the Falls Road by Denis McCullough but their plan to join with the Tyrone Volunteers and make their way to Galway collapsed when the

Tyrone men refused to move.

On the Monday afternoon the County Louth contingent under Sean MacEntee (afterwards a leading Fianna Fáil politician) had killed a policeman and a guards officer from among their prisoners. There was a low-level and soon abandoned operation against a police station in Galway while the Volunteers in Limerick on stand-by on Easter Sunday stood down on receiving MacNeill's countermand and, knowing of the loss of the *Aud*, ignored Pearse's final order. In Enniscorthy the local battalion took over the town on Tuesday morning and surrendered to the military on Vinegar Hill on the Friday. Cork mustered 1,000 men on Easter Sunday, but they went home after having received nine different sets of instructions, each new one contradicting the last.

One other event of the Tuesday has lived in infamy: a captain of the Royal Irish Rifles called Bowen-Colthurst arrested two journalists, Patrick McIntyre and Thomas Dickson and the well-known pacifist Francis Sheehy-Skeffington. None had had anything to do with the Rising, though Sheehy-Skeffington was trying to organise a citizens' band to prevent looting and his wife Hanna was a messenger in the GPO. The next morning on his own initiative Bowen-Colthurst had them shot, the bungled operation requiring two firing-squads. It was known that on the Tuesday evening while out on patrol and having Sheehy-Skeffington with him as a hostage he had deliberately shot a boy called Coade in Rathmines. A court-martial insisted upon by a senior officer Sir Francis Vane in spite of Castle inertia found Bowen-Colthurst of unsound mind, but Hanna Sheehy-Skeffington continued demands for further action until a Royal Commission made an apology and an offer of monetary compensation which she refused.

Wednesday saw the first Republican surrender when Heuston had to evacuate the Mendicity Institute which was nearest to Lowe's central chain of firepower. MacDonagh's men in Jacob's were holding out with few casualties but Ceannt in the South Dublin Union was under continuous fierce attack. The British heavy firepower was greatly improved by the fitting out of a boat, the *Helga*, as an artillery platform. She anchored in the Liffey near the North Wall and soon demolished Liberty Hall and removed the top storey of the GPO. She continued to pound the city centre until Sackville Street was reduced to rubble and the gold lettering on the flag above the beleaguered Post Office had turned dark brown.

Yet it was on the same day that the Volunteers had their most impressive military success and learnt many lessons for the future. Reinforcements had arrived at Kingstown in the shape of two companies of the Sherwood Foresters. They were welcomed by the majority of Dubliners as saviours but consisted of new recruits, most of whom had been in the army for less than three months. They came from Nottingham as part of the deadly 'comrades' recruiting initiative which meant that whole streets, factory workshops, village populations all joined up together and died together. The gossip about the city was that some of them thought they had landed in France. One column made their way safely along the Stillorgan Road to the Royal Hospital. As the other marched along Northumberland Road towards Mount Street Bridge to cross the Grand Canal they were caught in crossfire from de Valera's outposts. It took many hours for them to force their way across the canal and at the cost of four officers killed and fourteen wounded and 216 ORs killed or seriously injured. The total number of Volunteers in the engagement was put as two in a house in Haddington Road, three in Northumberland Road and seven in Clanwilliam House on Mount Street. The fire was so persistent and so rapid that the rifles of the insurgents were cooled with oil from sardine tins, probably their main rations. One of the men in 25 Northumberland Road, Lieutenant Michael Malone, was killed and of the seven who held Clanwilliam House from noon till 8 p.m. three died. The rest, covered by sniper fire, retreated to Boland's only after the house had been set on fire.

On Thursday it was realised that all lines of communication between headquarters and the other positions were finally cut. Connolly on reconnaissance in the streets around the Post Office, now hardly defendable, was shot twice in the leg and in the various Volunteer emplacements the talk was of evacuation, if not actual surrender. Brugha was seriously wounded in an attack on the South Dublin Union but by sheer ferocity he and the other defenders beat the British back.

Birrell returned on the Friday accompanying General Sir John Maxwell, who was to take over as C-in-C. Maxwell was to say rashly to Lord Wimbourne, the Lord Lieutenant, 'I am going to ensure that there will be no treason whispered for a hundred years.' His first announcement on arrival was: 'If necessary I shall not hesitate to destroy all buildings within any area occupied by the rebels.' This was indicative of the wisdom and delicacy with which he would handle the aftermath of surrender. He and Lowe had now 20,000 British troops deployed and the city centre was cordoned off. It was a day of attrition with shellfire growing more and more accurate, streets raked with machine-gun bullets, and charging and dismantling of barricades the main military activity.

Pearse had issued another communiqué at 9.30 a.m. reassuring those who had fought that they had 'redeemed Dublin from many shames, and made her name splendid among the names of cities.' He then dismissed the women and girls, shaking hands with each as they left. By evening the GPO was on fire and the Cumann na mBan members who were still on duty and wounded were moved back to Jervis Street Hospital. The remaining Volunteers decided to make a dash through Moore Street to Great Britain Street but they did not know that Henry Street was continuously under British fire mainly from the Rotunda. The O'Rahilly volunteered to reconnoitre Henry Street to see if it was worth trying to reach Moore Street. Before he left he made sure that thirteen prisoners who had been held in the GPO were safe before heading out. He was shot in Moore Lane. (He was one of the men whom Yeats remembered with typical affection. He had delivered Mac-Neill's orders to Kerry and Limerick but headed for Dublin himself, and in the ballad 'The O'Rahilly' Yeats has him say to Pearse and Connolly:

'Because I helped to wind the clock
I come to hear it strike.'

Most of the rest of the men in the Post Office were got out in spite of the slaughtering fire, MacDermott and Plunkett managing to get a van pulled across Henry Street. Three women who had stayed got safely across to Moore Street, as did Pearse, though in his dash he stumbled and the others thought he had been hit. Connolly, now on a stretcher, was also carried to safety. There were seventeen casualties during the operation and when the others settled into 16 Moore Street they were able to break through the walls of houses to give them a frontage on Great Britain Street. It was clear to even the most sanguine that the fighting was about over.

There was to be one other operation on that Friday which has become part of the mythology. Thomas Ashe, with Richard Mulcahy (who took command of the Free State forces after the death of Michael Collins in August 1922) as lieutenant, engaged a force of the paramilitary RIC at Ashbourne on the road to Slane about thirteen miles from Dublin. Ashe was from County Kerry and was principal of Lusk national school. He became commander of the County

Meath Volunteers and his ambush was an anticipation of the tactics that were to be employed during the Anglo-Irish War that would start three years later. A party of forty RIC men led by a chief inspector were on their way to relieve the barracks at Ashbourne and they were effectively ambushed at a crossroads about a mile north of the town. The fight lasted for five hours and when the police ran out of ammunition they surrendered. Eight had been killed and fifteen wounded. Ashe's company had up till then moved freely about the county attacking barracks and doing what they could to disrupt communications.

The Battle of Ashbourne and the Battle of Mount Street were really the only effective encounters of the week. They would be studied by the next set of insurgents, especially by Michael Collins, who took command of what was now called Sinn Féin on the death of Ashe from pneumonia brought on by force feeding during his hunger strike in Mountjoy in 1917.

The Rising was effectively finished and by the Saturday morning the decision to seek terms from Lowe had been made. It is said that it was the shooting of a publican and his family while running out of one of the houses carrying a white flag that persuaded Pearse that it was time to call a halt. Connolly, who with the exception of MacBride was the only one with military experience and who had supervised whatever minimal tactics were devised in the Post Office, agreed. He had said on the Monday, 'We are going out to be slaughtered,' and probably felt that too many others were being needlessly slaughtered as well.

A Cumann na mBan nurse, Elizabeth O'Farrell, carried a white flag and this message to the British barricade at Great Britain Street:

> The Commandant-General of the Irish Republican Army wishes to treat with the Commandant-General of the British forces in Ireland.

Lowe demanded an unconditional surrender and at 3.30 p.m. Pearse, wearing a greatcoat and a Boer War slouch hat handed his sword to Lowe. (The grainy photograph showing the surrender, if not the actual passing of the sword, also shows Lowe's aide-de-camp, his eighteen-year old son, Lt John Lowe (1898–1988) who as John Loder became a Hollywood leading-man, married Hedy Lamarr and wrote a very funny autobiography *Hollywood Hussar* (1977).) At 3.45 he signed the typed order of stand-down:

> In order to prevent the further slaughter of Dublin citizens, and in the hope of saving the lives of our followers now surrounded and hopelessly outnumbered, the members of the Provisional Government present at Headquarters have agreed to unconditional surrender, and the Commandants of the various districts in the City and County will order their commands to lay down their arms.

The order had to be countersigned by Connolly since the Citizen Army recognised no leader but him:

> I agree to these conditions for the men only under my command in the Moore

Street district and for the men in the
Stephen's Green command.

At nine o'clock that evening the Volunteers,
apart from those in Jacob's and Boland's and the
South Dublin Union, marched from Moore
Street along Sackville Street and dumped their
arms at the foot of the five-year-old Parnell
statue. Then they were made to lie on the grass
in the Rotunda grounds. Later that evening a
British officer called Lee Wilson amused himself
by stripping Clarke naked and parading him in
view of the nurses who were looking out the
windows of the hospital. Clarke, in his sixtieth
year, was by the standards of the time an elderly
man and it was a particularly cruel thing to do
to a person of known prudery. Watching the
humiliation was Michael Collins, who was able
to announce five years later: 'We got him [Lee
Wilson] today in Gorey.'

MacDonagh, with most of his force intact,
refused to accept the order until he had spoken
to Pearse, a prisoner in Richmond Barracks, and
then had difficulty in persuading Ceannt to
surrender. His addition to Pearse's order read:

> On consultation with Commandant
> Ceannt and other officers I have decided
> to agree to unconditional surrender also.

The greatest difficulty was experienced by de Valera at the garrison at Boland's mills. The defences had not been breached – unlike most of the other emplacements it was a tactical building – and the men were prepared for a much longer siege. When they did obey the order, many broke their rifles in dismay on the ground.

The most notable thing about the city that day was the ending of the noise of the fighting as Brighid Lyons Thornton, who was one of the Cumann na mBan members in the Four Courts, described it in *Curious Journey*:

> And then Saturday morning, louder than
> all the noise was the silence that descended
> upon the city.

She also recalled that after the surrender:

... some of the Church Street priests came in and lambasted us with abuse all night for doing what we did. They disapproved highly of the rebellion, of the damage to the city and the people who were killed and whose homes were burned.

The Church could not approve the Rising since it met none of the moral criteria, and the Dublin priests shared the feelings of dismay and anger of the majority population. A number of Capuchin fathers, Augustine, Columbus, Aloysius, Sebastian and Albert, were allowed to minister to those condemned to death, and Aloysius and Augustine travelled from post to post in Lowe's car, which he had put at their disposal, as bona fides that Pearse had signed the surrender. Yet one initially reluctant curate from the Pro-Cathedral, Fr John Flanagan, became a kind of unofficial chaplain in the Post Office, hearing confessions, giving extreme unction to the dying and helping the Volunteers move to the Moore Street post on the Friday, giving them absolution before the reckless evacuation. He also cheered the men up by eating chicken with them on the Friday.

As such things go the casualties were light: of the Volunteers sixty-four dead excluding those who would later be executed; 134 soldiers killed or dead of wounds while 318 were wounded; seventeen policemen from the DMP and the RIC, the latter mainly at Ashbourne, and five 'Gorgeous Wrecks'. It was the civilians who suffered most with at least 220 killed and wounded in excess of 600. The centre of the city was rubble and indeed in the rough ellipse formed by the Circular Roads many buildings were damaged. The fury of the populace was vented early; Brighid Lyons Thornton describes how the women, led by the rebel countess, needed the protection of the army as they were marched towards Kilmainham from the Four Courts.

> Never did I see such savage women. A lot of them were getting the separation allowance because their husbands were off fighting in France and they thought their livelihood would be taken away because of what we did.

The role of Cumann na mBan members was generally caring for the wounded and preparing food for the men but not all the women were content to be helpmeets. Fifteen of them, members of the Citizen Army, fought beside the men in St Stephen's Green and the College of Surgeons. These included Countess Markievicz who had trained Na Fianna, the boys brigade, who were drilled and taught the use of arms (most of them were sent home 'with a kick in the pants' and not interned; Sean Lemass, later the great moderniser of Ireland, was one shown that rough mercy) and as commander of a battalion of troops she engaged in hostile fire. Margaret Skinnider (c. 1893–1971), the Glasgow feminist, was bravest (or rashest), tried to blow up the Shelbourne and was a daring rooftop sniper. She held logically that the political and social equality that she was struggling for required equality of risk. A crack shot, she was wounded in an attack on a machine-gun post and arrested from St Vincent's Hospital. Kathleen Lynn (1874-1955), the daughter of an Anglican canon and one of the first women to graduate in medicine from the Royal University, was the

Citizen Army chief medical officer and negotiated the surrender of the City Hall emplacement. Madeleine ffrench-Mullen (1890–1944) who ran the medical post in St Stephen's Green, was to join with Dr Lynn in founding St Ultan's Infant Hospital in Charlemont Street in 1919. A sixteen-year-old Molly O'Reilly (c. 1900–1950) was the City Hall dispatch carrier.

In light of this level of participation it was perfectly appropriate that it should have been a woman who parlayed with the officer in charge at the barricade in Great Britain Street. Seventy women in all were arrested and Markievicz was condemned to death but reprieved. Her colleague Helen Molony, the trade-union organiser and Abbey actress who had taken part in the attack on Dublin Castle, was also interned. One heroine of the Rising was not in Dublin but played her part in Kerry, making arrangements for the reception of the *Aud*, This was Kathleen Timoney (c. 1889–1972) whose baby, christened Pearse, of course, was born on 3 May 1916!

Birrell in one of his last dispatches had advised Asquith and the Liberal cabinet that the Rising was not an *Irish* rebellion: 'It would be a pity if *post facto* it became one.' Birrell's advice was usually sound and just as usually ignored. He resigned as chief secretary on 3 May when with deaths of Pearse, Clarke and MacDonagh Maxwell had taken the first steps to make it very much an *Irish* rebellion – if not *the* Irish rebellion.

5

THE EXECUTIONS

It is hard to determine exactly when the mood of betrayal and rage began to change. The surrender was followed by wholesale arrests of many who had had no connection with the Rising. 3,430 men and seventy-nine women were arrested but of these 1,424 men and all but five of the women were released within six weeks. These five included Kathleen Clarke, soon to be the widow of Tom Clarke and designated to lead the IRB should the members of the military council be killed. One-hundred-and-seventy men and Countess Markievicz were imprisoned while 1,836 men and five women were interned, mainly at Frongoch in present-day Gwyned.

Asquith had agreed that the 'ringleaders' be dealt with in the 'most severe way possible' and

Redmond had acquiesced. John Dillon disagreed with his leader and kept haranguing Maxwell about the short-sightedness of his policy. In fact ninety death sentences were passed and seventy-five of them commuted. What made the disposal of 'the ringleaders' so appalling and politically unwise was the piecemeal nature of the executions. On Wednesday 3 May, a mere four days after the surrender, the official announcement was made:

> Three signatories of the notice proclaiming the Irish Republic, P. H. Pearse, T. MacDonagh, and T. J. Clarke have been tried by Field Court Martial and sentenced to death. The sentence having been duly confirmed the three above-mentioned men were shot this morning.

The first of the martyrs were shot at dawn in the yard of Kilmainham; the usual humane decencies were not observed in that while they received Holy Communion the priest was not allowed to be with them at the end in spite of his promise. A tiny crack appeared in the granite façade of Maxwell's harshness in that Mrs Pearse was allowed to visit her second son William and the widow of Thomas Clarke her brother, Edward Daly, both due to be shot the next day along with Michael O'Hanrahan and the terminally-ill Joseph Plunkett. He was married to the artist Grace Gifford by candlelight, because of a power failure, in the prison chapel at midnight a few hours before the dawn execution. The prison chaplain Fr Eugene McCarthy officiated. None of the bodies were allowed burial in consecrated ground but were burned with quicklime, the common means of disposal of convicted murderers. The others might conceivably have been regarded as 'ringleaders' but Willie Pearse was shot simply because he was Patrick's brother.

The simultaneous announcement that seventeen other court-martial sentences had been commuted to penal service did nothing to mitigate the perceived cruelty of the military reaction. If anything it seemed part of a cold game of cat-and-mouse. Redmond, already regretting his stance, kept appealing for clemency in the Commons and visited Asquith daily. Asquith wired Maxwell that there should be no more executions but he was ignored and Redmond did not, as he had threatened, resign. The Liberal party was showing its usual inability to challenge the War Office and the senior military establishment. John MacBride was shot on 5 May in spite of his total ignorance of the IRB's intentions before Easter Monday (he wasn't trustworthy enough). He had, however, told the court that he had stared down the barrels of British rifles far too often in the past to be afraid of death. And though he was in Yeats's eyes 'a drunken vain glorious lout' he too was numbered in the song. The flamboyant reputation of his estranged wife who had figured in Castle records for more than a decade may have played its part in his selection for death.

The executions (and the commutations) continued in spite of near-frantic appeals by members of the Irish party. Maxwell who with military logic regarded the Rising as a German plot to discommode Britain on the eve of the great putsch on the Somme was coming under pressure from southern unionists to be even more draconian. Colbert, Ceannt, Mallin and Heuston were shot on 8 May and Connolly and

MacDermott on the twelfth. The deliberateness of the executions and the stringing out of them over ten days was described later by the Countess of Fingall as a 'stream of blood coming from beneath a closed door'. Maxwell conceded to Asquith that Connolly's and MacDermott's would be the last, although no one outside government circles knew this. They could not be sure that the blood had stopped. Asquith had announced in the Commons on 10 May that thirteen executions had taken place, seventy-three people had been sentenced to penal servitude and six to hard labour while 1,706 were deported.

The prisoners were treated badly, especially as they were being transported to English jails in Stafford, Wakefield, Lewes, Knutsford, Glasgow, Perth. Later they were transferred to the Frongoch internment camp. Their spirits were generally high and 'A Soldier's Song' was bawled out at every excuse. They were gratified too that as they were marched to their less than palatial transports (often cattle boats) they were cheered by the people. The women who had pelted them with eggs and tomatoes in April now came forward to kiss them and fill their pockets with gifts.

It was not only at home that opinion was changing. The *Manchester Guardian*, the leading liberal paper of the day, declared that the executions 'were becoming an atrocity'. The British Ambassador in Washington, who had reassured the cabinet that public opinion was against the Rising, had a different story to tell after news of the executions became known. The fact that many of those who had taken part were poets as an instant anthology *Poems of the Irish Revolutionary Brotherhood* (1916), published in Boston, clearly showed, undermined any attempt to write them off as heartless gunmen. Publication of substantial work by Pearse, Plunkett and MacDonagh soon after their deaths had the effect on the British reading public of having to take what they said seriously. World opinion was turning against the British and too late they did what they could to limit the damage. Just before Christmas 600 internees who were untried were welcomed home with country-wide jubilation (except in the predictable areas of the North) and by 16 June 1917 all the prisoners were released, including de Valera,

MacNeill (whose arrest and that of Griffith provided clear evidence of the wrongheadedness of Maxwell's policy) and Markievicz.

It was clear that the country's freedom from treason would not last the hundred years prophesied by Maxwell and it was largely his own fault. Other reasons for the country's change of heart were a general increase of anglophobia and the growing conviction that the Liberals were not to be trusted. The dignity of the Volunteers who had taken part in the Rising and their undoubted heroism also played their part. The mass of the Irish population felt that they had been honoured rather than disgraced and when the story of Sheehy-Skeffington and the apparent early unconcern of the military authorities became known there was general affront.

And so in spite of all efforts the Rising achieved its purpose; the country was united and militant and through no fault of its worthy leader Redmondism was dead. The full extent of the support for Sinn Féin was evident in the immediately postwar general election when the party won seventy-three of the country's 105 seats to the Home Rule party's six. The time of imprisonment had been for the Volunteers (and those who had been arrested without cause) a crash course in Irish culture, nationality and revolution. And under new and more ruthless leaders that revolution came. Elizabeth Bowen summed up the feeling of the time in her history of the Shelbourne (1951):

> Executions, wholesale arrests, deportations savoured to Ireland of Cromwellian reprisals; they were to combine to plough 1916 deep in among the other race-memories in the country's heart. There was to be much more of it to come.

Yet the Irish are a resilient people and she could not help adding:

> As for the Shelbourne, it woke from a bad dream. Sandbags gone, soldiers out, staff back, it returned to normal in (virtually) the twinkling of an eye.

6

AFTERMATH

The events of Easter Week have been the subject of much writing, both hagiographic and revisionist. The proclamation, the communiqués, the statement of surrender, Pearse's poems, especially those written before his execution, became a series of near-sacred texts. The accounts of Plunkett's marriage and the ten minutes that the couple were allowed together, MacDonagh's dying 'like a prince', as the presiding officers recalled, Connolly's execution strapped to a chair because of his gangrenous leg, the commutation of de Valera's death sentence (wrongly believed to have resulted from American diplomatic intervention, though Redmond and Dillon who secured it from Asquith may have emphasised in the negotiations that he had been born of a Spanish father and an Irish mother in Manhattan), all combined to make a heady mythology that became the staple learning of the children of the Free State.

The nature of the Rising and the British response made the Anglo-Irish War inevitable and its greater brutality was realised to be of the nature of such warfare. The Civil War which followed and which was if anything more grisly also had its roots in 1916. It set in motion the process which would result in Saorstát Éireann and in time give most of the Irish people an approximation of what Pearse, Collins and Griffith had fought for. But it also gave respectability to the partitioning of the country which though unwanted even by the unionists was given to them on the best possible terms. The losers, the ones on whom the Rising inflicted the most grievous injury, were the nationalists of the Six Counties, chosen with precision to make the province governable as a one-party state with Catholics the victims of severe and institutionalised apartheid. It is one of the ironies of the years that followed Partition that nowhere were the icons of 1916 more devoutly worshipped than in Tyrone and Derry City and in West Belfast.

The men and women of 1916 were on the whole admirable, idealistic and civilised, and their policies in so far as their implications were understood liberal and non-sectarian. Their self-sacrifice was understood by them at least to be no more that a glorious statement of belief. They did what they could to keep their fight honourable and temporary. Yet the subsequent coarsening of their ideals in the minds of some who came later did them less than justice. The seventy-fifth anniversary of the Rising in 1991 was a notably less vocal and less confident affair than the fiftieth. A majority of people could not help contrast the five or six days of glory with thirty years of murderous attrition in Northern Ireland, and, what would have hurt Pearse and MacDonagh more, effectively sectarian conflict, for all the doublethink of the apologists for the continuance of the 'armed struggle'. The colder eye turned upon the events and personalities of Easter Week not just by historians but by most Irish people was rooted in the argument: if the violence and terror and cruelty are the logical outcome of the Volunteer ideals then perhaps they were always fundamentally flawed.

Another dubious legacy, some argue, is the embracing and advocacy of the ultimate sacrifice *ar son na hÉireann*. This was expressed succinctly by Sir Arnold Bax (1883–1953), in a banned poem 'A Dublin Ballad – 1916':

To all true Irishmen on earth
Arrest and death come late or soon.

The actions of the Rising were taken and its principles formulated when by late-twentieth-century standards the lives of young men were cheap. By the time a second apocalyptic war had finished, the more pragmatic felt that perhaps living for Ireland was preferable – and perhaps more difficult – than dying for her. It also imposed upon certain families reared in an uncritical Republican tradition a kind of responsibility to look for England's difficulty and continue the struggle. The resurrection of the IRA at the time of the civil rights agitation of 1968-9 may be directly ascribed to this tradition.

It is difficult to assess whether the result of Easter Week was disastrous for the final settlement of the perennial Irish Question. It hardened unionist attitudes, though some wondered if they could be any harder; it let the British Government off the hook, with the sound-hearted but indecisive Asquith having to give place to the brilliant but essentially unsympathetic Lloyd George. He would not confront the absolutism of Carson and Craig and the hot breath of Bonar Law and his baying Conservative and Unionist party reminded him how unrewarding Irish affairs had always been for any British career politician. His reputation for wizardry was at stake and the success of the Treaty negotiations, with the weary Irish delegation unwittingly allowing themselves to be diverted from the hardest nut of all to crack, allowed him to defer the problem of what Churchill memorably metaphorised as 'the dreary steeples of Tyrone and Fermanagh' for later generations to solve.

Yet in spite equally of detractors and interpreters a reappraisal of the men and women of 1916 leaves the researcher with affection if not total approval. It is vain to try to argue that they would have not countenanced the things done in their name; as with most other historical events and personalities later generations reinvent them to suit their own propaganda or psychological needs. They are remembered in Kilmainham, in the Pearse Museum in Rathfarnham and in the 1916 room in the National Museum in Kildare Street. The sight of many personal possessions, Markievicz's Mauser pistol, Pearse's almost unused wig and gown, Connolly's blood-stained shirt (now removed for conservation purposes), all those splendid green uniforms, has a remarkable effect on all but the totally unimaginative. The places associated with Easter Week have a right to their positions as national shrines and a country could have a worse set of revolutionary heroes; there is a lot less painting out of warts required with these than with the equivalents in other countries born in revolt. The line from 'The Mother', possibly Pearse's best known poem, insists upon attention, its ambivalences forgotten:

My sons were faithful, and they fought.

BIOGRAPHICAL INDEX

Thomas Ashe (1885–1917) was born in Lispole, County Kerry and trained as a teacher, becoming the principal of Lusk NS in north County Dublin. He was active in the Gaelic League and was County Meath commander of the Volunteers. He featured in its greatest military success at the ambush of an RIC detachment at Ashbourne on the Friday of Easter Week. He was sentenced to life imprisonment but released in 1917. Rearrested, he organised a hunger-strike in Mountjoy for political status for Sinn Féin prisoners and died of pneumonia brought on by force-feeding.

Herbert Henry Asquith (1852-1928) was Liberal prime minister (1908–14) and led the war coalition until he was superseded by Lloyd George in 1916. The Rising found him at his weakest politically and he allowed Maxwell* too much power in its aftermath.

Piaras Beaslaí (1881–1965) was born in Liverpool and moved to Dublin in 1904. He was active in the Gaelic League and did much to politicise it. He commanded the forces in the North King Street area during the Rising.

Augustine Birrell (1850–1933) was born near Liverpool. He was chief secretary for Ireland (1907–16) and was tireless in his efforts to keep the spirit of the Home Rule Bill alive. He resigned after the Rising and saw all his sound advice wantonly ignored.

Cathal Brugha (1874–1922) was born Charles Burgess in Dublin. He joined the Gaelic League in 1899 and the Volunteers in 1913. He was second-in-command to Eamonn Ceannt* in the South Dublin Union in Easter week and so badly wounded on the Thursday that he was permanently crippled. He was a strong opponent of the Treaty and was shot in Talbot Street in the second week of the Civil War.

Roger Casement (1864–1916) was born in Dublin of County Antrim parents and educated at Ballymena Academy. He joined the British consular service in 1892 and was knighted for his reports on human rights violations in the Congo and the Amazon basin. He joined the Gaelic League in 1904 and the Volunteers in 1913. Arrested off the County Kerry coast at

Easter 1916 on his return from Germany, he was hanged in Pentonville on 3 August 1916, having been received into the Catholic Church.

Eamonn Ceannt (1881–1916) was born Edmund Kent in Glenamaddy, County Galway. He commanded the South Dublin Union, a post that was fiercely attacked but did not fall. He was bitterly disappointed by Pearse*'s surrender. He was shot by firing squad on 8 May 1916.

Kathleen Clarke (1879–1972) was born Daly in Limerick, where she married Tom Clarke* on his release from prison in 1898. She became formal head of the IRB when the leaders were executed and initiated an Irish Volunteers Dependants Fund within a few days of the executions. She helped to organise Cumann na mBan in 1921, opposed the Treaty and was Dublin's first woman Lord Mayor (in 1939).

Thomas James Clarke (1857–1916) was born in the Isle of Wight of Irish parents and brought up in South Africa and Dungannon. He went to America in 1871 and joined Clan na Gael, returning to England on a dynamiting mission in 1883. He was arrested and sentenced to life imprisonment, of which he served fifteen years under severe conditions. He was released in 1898 but unable to find work, returned to the US. His return to Dublin in 1907 was with the deliberate intention of reviving the IRB. A signatory of the Proclamation, he served in the GPO during Easter Week and was executed with Pearse* and MacDonagh* on 3 May 1916.

Con Colbert was a member of Na Fianna and later joined the IRB and the Irish Volunteers. In the Easter Rising he commanded the post in Watkin's Brewery in Ardee Street. He was executed in Kilmainham on 8 May 1916.

Michael Collins (1890–1922) was in the GPO during Easter Week and was interned but released in December 1916. He organised the intelligence service that was so important during the Anglo-Irish war. He was a reluctant delegate to the Treaty negotiations, commanded the Free State forces at the beginning of the Civil War and was killed in an ambush in County Cork on 22 August 1922.

James Connolly (1868–1916) was born in Edinburgh of Irish parents. Having been a socialist labour organiser in Ireland and the US, he returned to Ireland in 1910 and was the worker's leader while Larkin was imprisoned during the 1913 lock-out. He formed the Citizen Army, convinced that Ireland was ripe for an armed socialist revolt. He was persuaded to join with the IRB and as the leader with some experience was made military commander during the Rising. His execution on 12 May 1916 marked the end of the judicial killings.

Edward Daly (1891–1916) was born in Limerick into a noted Republican family. His sister Kathleen* married Tom Clarke*. He joined the Volunteers in 1914 and commanded the Four Courts garrison during Easter Week. He was executed in Kilmainham on 4 May 1916.

Eamon de Valera (1882–1975) joined the Gaelic League in 1908 and the Volunteers in 1913. He reluctantly joined the IRB but maintained a lifelong distrust of secret organisations. He was sentenced to death but reprieved thanks to the efforts of Redmond* and Dillon*. His greatest achievement was the politicisation of republican-ism in the founding of the Fianna Fáil party. Like many Irish revolutionaries he was a con-servative politician and a devout Catholic. He led four governments for a total of twenty-one years and served as president for two terms (1959–1973).

John Devoy (1842–1928) was born in Kill, County Kildare, and served in both the French Foreign Legion and the British Army, where he became a Fenian spy. He helped in the rescue of the Fenian 'chief' James Stephens (1825–1901) from Richmond Jail in 1865 and, given fifteen years imprisonment for organising 'cells', was amnestied after serving five years on condition of his living outside the United Kingdom. He led Clan na Gael and supported all anti-British movements thereafter, including the Land War and the Rising. He died penniless in Atlantic City.

John Dillon (1851–1927) was an often violent supporter of Parnell but led the anti-Parnellites after the split. In the aftermath of the Rising he was active in pleading for an end to the arrests and executions.

Madeleine ffrench-Mullen (1880–1944) was a member of Inghinidhe na hÉireann and children's editor of its newspaper *Bean na hÉireann* (1908–11). A member of the Citizen Army she was in charge of the medical post in the

College of Surgeons, and in 1919 helped found St Ultan's Infant Hospital with her friend Kathleen Lynn*.

Arthur Griffith (1871–1922) was a member of the Gaelic League and the IRB, and in 1906 founded Sinn Féin, an organisation which emphasised Irish self-sufficiency and passive resistance. He opposed the Home Rule Bill, joined the Volunteers in 1913 and although not a participant was arrested after the Rising. He led the Treaty delegation in 1921 but died soon after the beginning of the Civil War.

Sean Heuston (1891–1916) joined the Volunteers in 1913 and led a contingent of Na Fianna to bring arms from the *Asgard* safely to Dublin. He was in command of the Mendicity Institute but had to surrender on the Wednesday of Easter Week. He was executed in Kilmainham on 8 May 1916.

Thomas Kent (*c.* 1867–1916) was a Volunteer who awaited the countermanding of MacNeill's orders in his home in Cork. On 2 May 1916 his house was surrounded by the RIC attempting to arrest him; he and his brothers resisted, holding out for three hours, during which a head constable and one of the Kent brothers were shot. He was executed in Cork seven days later.

Bulmer Hobson (1883–1969) with Denis McCullough* founded the Dungannon clubs which helped to resuscitate the IRB. He was also a member of the GAA, the Gaelic League, Griffith*'s Sinn Féin and founder of the Ulster Literary Theatre. He disapproved of the planned Rising and was kept in detention until the fighting had begun.

Brig. General William Henry Muir Lowe (1861–*c*. 1940) was the commander of British forces in Dublin during Easter Week, until Maxwell* became military governor on the Friday. He received Pearse*'s surrender and was mentioned in dispatches, being promoted to the honorary rank of major-general.

Kathleen Florence Lynn (1874–1955) was a suffragist and feminist. She joined the Citizen Army and became its chief medical officer, negotiating the surrender of City Hall. She became an executive member of Sinn Féin in 1918 and opposed the Treaty.

John MacBride (1865–1916) joined the IRB and worked with Michael Cusack (1847–1906) in the formation of the GAA. He served as a major with the Boers in the Boer War. He was not a member of the Volunteers but the offer of his services was gladly accepted by MacDonagh*, who made him second-in-command at Jacob's. He was shot by firing squad in Kilmainham on 5 May 1916.

Sean MacDermott (1884–1916) while working as a barmen in Belfast met Bulmer Hobson*, under whose influence he joined the IRB and in 1907 became a full-time organiser for Sinn Féin. He was probably the best organiser and had the most determined mind of all the leaders, devising with Plunkett* a forged document that suggested that the authorities were about to proscribe the Volunteers. He fought in the GPO and on 12 May 1916 was the penultimate insurgent to be executed.

Thomas MacDonagh (1878–1916) joined the Gaelic League in 1901 and helped Pearse* to establish St Enda's in 1908. He was a founder member of the Irish Volunteers in 1913 and its director of training. He joined the IRB on cooption to the military council and commanded the garrison at Jacob's factory in Bishop Street.

He was executed on 3 May 1916, along with Pearse* and Clarke*.

Eoin MacNeill (1867–1945) was professor of early Irish history in UCD (1908–45) and was a leading force in the founding of the Irish Volunteers. He was opposed to the Rising as planned and tried with some success to prevent the Volunteers form mobilising. Later he supported the Treaty, becoming minister of education in the first Free State Dáil.

Sean MacEntee (1889–1984) as commander of the County Louth division was held responsible for the deaths of two prisoners. He was condemned to death but the sentence was commuted to life imprisonment. Released in 1917, he fought in the Anglo-Irish war and opposed the Treaty. A founder member of Fianna Fáil, he held many cabinet posts, his last as Minister for Health (1957–65).

Michael Mallin (1880–1916) was born in Dublin. He was in command in St Stephen's Green but soon realised that an occupied Shelbourne Hotel would dominate the fire and the company retired to the College of Surgeons. He was shot in Kilmainham on 8 May 1916.

Constance Markievicz (1868–1927) was born Gore-Booth in London and brought up at Lissadell, County Sligo, where her Protestant ascendancy family had extensive estates. She joined the Citizen Army and was second-in-command to Mallin* in the St Stephen's Green sector. She was condemned to death but on the sentence's commutation to penal servitude for life was kept in Aylesbury prison in Buckinghamshire until the amnesty in 1917. In the 1918 general election she was elected for St Patrick's division, Dublin – the first woman MP – but did not take her seat. She opposed the Treaty and toured America to enlist support for the Republican cause. She died shortly after election to the Dáil as a Fianna Fáil TD.

General Sir John Maxwell (1859–1929) became C-in-C Ireland, superseding Lowe on 28 April 1916. He insisted upon a complete and urgent defeat for the Volunteers. Instigating martial law, he was the only authority in Ireland for the next critical month and the policy of paced executions and massive arrests was his. When the British government realised the effects of his policies they did what they could to mitigate them.

Helena Molony (1884–1967) was born in Dublin and joined Inghinidhe na hÉireann in 1903, becoming editor of its newspaper *Bean na hÉireann* in 1908. She was given the task by Connolly* in 1915 of organising the Irish Women Workers Union (IWWU) and was with the City Hall command during Easter Week. She was released in December 1916, continued her trade-union work and was president of ICTU (1922–3).

Denis McCullough (1883–1968) was a close associate of Bulmer Hobson* in the founding of the Dungannon Clubs and the Ulster Literary Theatre, and became president of the IRB. He helped to organise the Volunteers in Ulster and was arrested in 1916 and interned at Frongoch.

Richard Mulcahy (1886–1971) joined the IRB and the Volunteers and was Ashe*'s second-in-command at Ashbourne. He was interned at Frongoch and later became chief-of-staff of the IRA. During the Civil War he became GOC of the Free State army after the death of Collins in 1922* and thereafter was active in Dáil politics, being one of the founders of Fine Gael.

Jeremiah O'Donovan Rossa (1831–1915) was born in Rosscarbery, County Cork, the 'Rossa' being added to his name for effect. He was one of the early Fenian organisers, founding the Phoenix Society of Skibbereen in 1858. He had the usual Fenian career of nationalist activity, 'seditious' journalism, appalling treatment in British prisons and political exile. Because of his abrasive personality and alcoholism he was often at odds with the other members of Clan na Gael. At his funeral in Glasnevin, Pearse* claimed him as a symbol of IRB continuity.

Michael O'Hanrahan (1877–1916) was born in New Ross, County Wexford. He joined the Volunteers in 1913 and was with MacDonagh* in Jacob's factory during the Rising. He was executed on 4 May 1916.

The O'Rahilly (1875–1916) was born Michael Joseph Rahilly in Ballylongford, County Kerry. He was a member of Sinn Féin and joined the Volunteers in 1913, becoming its director of arms. He helped MacNeill* call off the Rising but went to Dublin himself. He was killed during the retreat from the GPO to Moore Street on the Friday of Easter Week.

Patrick Henry Pearse (1879–1916) joined the Gaelic League in 1895 and incorporated many of its ideals and techniques in his school, St Enda's, begun in 1908. He had been editor of *An Claidheamh Soluis* (1903–9) and had already begun in his writings to talk of a cleansing blood sacrifice which would restore the quick heart of Irish nationalism. He was commander-in-chief of the forces in the Rising, president of the provisional government, part-author with Connolly* and MacDonagh* (and one of the signatories) of the Proclamation which he read to a largely uninterested Dublin audience on Easter Monday and the person who agreed to unconditional surrender on Saturday 29 April 1916. He was the first to be executed four days later.

William Pearse (1881–1916) was born in Dublin, the brother of Patrick* whom he greatly admired. He was a fine sculptor and art master at St Enda's. He was a captain in the GPO but in no way involved in the planning of the Rising. His execution on 4 May 1916 was unquestionably due to the notoriety of his brother.

Joseph Mary Plunkett (1887–1916) was born in Dublin. He joined the Volunteers and was one of the first to be a member of the military council. He tried to assist Casement* in Germany in a quest for arms in 1915 but concealed the fact that Casement had strongly advised against a rising. He was in the GPO during Easter Week and executed on 4 May after a prison marriage to the artist Grace Gifford.

John Redmond (1856–1918) was born in County Wexford. He became chairman of the Nationalist party in 1900, having healed the rift caused by the fall of Parnell. Holding the balance in the Commons in 1910, he was able to get Asquith* to introduce a Home Rule Bill. He encouraged recruitment in the British Army and briefly supported Asquith*'s decision to make an example of the ringleaders of the Rising. His party was soundly defeated in the 1918 general election.

Francis Sheehy-Skeffington (1878–1916) was a well known supporter of such causes as women's suffrage, feminism and pacifism. He opposed the Rising and was arrested by Bowen-Colthurst and shot with Thomas Dickson and Patrick McIntyre in Portobello barracks on 26 April 1916.

Hanna Sheehy-Skeffington (1877–1946) was born Sheehy in Tipperary and educated at the Royal University. She married Francis Skeffington* and joined with him in the campaign for women's suffrage. She was a messenger at the GPO in 1916 and refused £10,000 compensation for the murder of her husband. She later served as a judge in the Dáil courts.

Margaret Skinnider (*c.* 1893–1971) was born in Glasgow. She was one of Markievicz*'s battalion at St Stephen's Green and as a suffragist and feminist insisted in active participation in the fighting. A crack shot, she was a successful sniper until she was badly wounded and eventually arrested in Saint Vincent's Hospital.

William Butler Yeats (1865–1939) was born in Dublin. He fell in love with Maud Gonne and through her was introduced to nationalism and IRB membership. He was deeply affected by the Rising, returning to it again and again in his poetry.

Leabharlann
Contae na Mhhe